Grandpa's Mumbling House

CONTENTS

The Visit	2
All Alone	7
Digging for Clams...	12
The Fog	16

By Deb Loughead

Illustrated by Stefan Messam

Grandpa's Mumbling House

The Visit

My grandpa lived by the sea, where booming waves bashed against the rocks all day.

I wasn't so sure I liked the seashore.

Grandpa was grizzled and old with grey hair that tangled like seaweed. His chin was stubbled with scratchy whiskers like a sea urchin and he smelled of the salty sea spray. He lived in a weathered old house that was faded and peeling from too much sunshine and salty air. It looked as if it had crept out of the sea, and now it loomed on the shore, gazing hungrily over the waves. Its wide window eyes seemed to be watching me, and its broad, sagging porch looked like a yawning mouth waiting to swallow me up. I wasn't so sure I liked that house. I wasn't so sure I liked Grandpa, either.

... I wasn't so

Imagery

Its wide window eyes seemed to be watching me ...

What picture do you see in your mind?

Alliteration = the repetition of the same letter or sound at the beginning of several words

Find an alliteration.

What other literary devices does the author use?

sure I liked Grandpa

Setting Analysis

How has the author created the setting of the story?

Literary Devices

Analogy = comparing two things that are similar in some way

Find an analogy.

What other literary devices does the author use?

One day, Mum told me I would be staying with Grandpa in that old house by the sea for a whole week – my very first visit since I was a little girl.

I didn't want to go to Grandpa's house . . .

I told my mum, even while she waited with me at the airport before I got on the plane. But she told me I had to go. She was going to be very busy moving all our things to a new house. And Dad was moving into a different house. Every time I thought about it, my insides felt as if they were crumpling up like a paper lunch bag.

When I arrived from the airport in a taxi, Grandpa came out to greet me. He wrapped his arms around me, and his stubbly whiskers scratched my face.

"How do you like being back at the seashore, Sophie?" he asked in a voice that rumbled like a storm.

"Fine, I guess," I said. Not so fine, I thought, as I squirmed away from that scratchy face.

"The sea can be your best friend or your worst enemy, Sophie," Grandpa told me. "Don't you forget that." Then he led me up the stairs into his dismal old house.

Question

hat do you
hink is going
n in Sophie's
amily?

...the sea can be your best friend
or your worst enemy

Inference

What can you
infer from . . .

Every time I thought about it,
my insides felt as if they were
crumpling up like a
paper lunch bag?

...what a friend the

6

Setting Analysis

How do you think the setting of Grandpa's house might be affecting Sophie?

All Alone

Inside the old house it was shadowy and unfamiliar, with dark furniture and saggy chairs and paintings of ships and oceans on every wall. At dinner time, Grandpa fried fish in a pan. He boiled potatoes and beans. Then we sat in the dim kitchen to eat. I missed home. I missed my own kitchen and my own table and my own food.

I missed my mum and dad.

"Tomorrow, Sophie, we're going to find out just what a friend the sea can be. We're going clam digging at the beach as soon as the tide goes out. Finish up your dinner and we can get ready for a good night's rest."

I picked a fish bone out of my mouth and put it on top of the bone pile on my plate. I wasn't so sure I liked fried fish.

Question

Why do you think Sophie wasn't enjoying her dinner?

At bedtime, I climbed into my
squeaky iron bed, pulled the covers
tight around my chin and lay there
staring into the dark, all alone.
There was a knock at the door.

"Can I come in?" asked Grandpa.

"I guess so," I told him.

Grandpa sat on a creaky wooden
rocker by the door and rocked in
the dark.

"I'm afraid this old house isn't too
quiet at night. But don't let the
sounds fool you, Sophie," he said.
"It's windy by the seashore, and it's
the wind that makes my old house
mumble and grumble in its sleep."

Then he sang me a song in his
rumbling voice. He told me that
it was a song he sang to me when
I was little and to my mother when
she slept in the very same bed.

"Row, row, row
your boat,
swiftly out
to sea.
Soon we'll catch
a mess of fish,
enough for you
and me."

...it's the wind th
mumble and

9

I closed my eyes and pretended I was asleep until Grandpa left the room. But I stayed awake for a long time after that, listening to the noises and blinking in the inky darkness.

The old house grumbled and groaned . . .

"Sophie, swiftly out to sea. Sophie, swiftly out to sea," the murmuring wind was saying.

I buried my head under my pillow and tried to forget that I was visiting Grandpa in his old house beside the sea where nothing felt like home.

I thought about my own house, far away in a distant city. A safe place where everything was familiar – the sunny yard, the tree house, the patio and the vegetable garden, my own cosy bed that never squeaked.

Literary Devices

metaphor
alliteration
simile
personification

Are there any?

My own bedroom, my own space.

I thought about all the noises I knew, such as the humming fridge and the squeaky clothes line, the creaky steps and the barking dog next door. No roaring waves, no murmuring wind, no faded old house that mumbled and grumbled in its sleep.

Then I thought about how all of that was changing now, how when I went back home it wouldn't be the same any more, how nothing would be familiar. And one tear slid in a sad, slow dribble down my cheek.

Setting Analysis

Sophie is comparing two settings – Grandpa's house and her house. How do the different settings affect her?

... the old house grumbled and groaned

Literary Devices

metaphor

alliteration

simile

personification

Are there any?

Setting Analysis

What is the mood
of the setting?
How is it
affecting
Sophie now?

Digging for Clams . . .

The next morning, after breakfast, I stood on a wide, flat beach, holding a shovel in one hand and a small bucket in the other. The foamy surf sparkled in the sunshine and seagulls did cartwheels over the waves. Grandpa stood beside me, staring at the sea.

"Tide's out now, Sophie. Time for digging clams," he said.

"How do you dig clams?" I asked.

"Am I going to like this?"

"You won't know until you try," said Grandpa. "Now keep your eyes on the beach and look for the tiny holes that clams make." He pointed to three holes in the sand, no bigger than worm holes in a garden.

"See. You find the holes and then you dig. Now crouch down here and watch what I do."

My grandpa pushed his shovel into the cool, wet sand and turned it over. Three streams of water squirted into the air like tiny fountains, and one of them sprayed me right in the eye. I yelped, and wiped away the salty water.

There's your clam," said Grandpa, laughing. "Next time don't get down so close and you won't get an eyeful!"

"You did that on purpose, didn't you, Grandpa?" I said. I tried to pretend I was mad, but I couldn't stop my lips from curling up into a smile.

I picked out the clams Grandpa had dug from their wet, sandy homes.

They sucked in their long tubular mouths when I dropped them into my clam bucket. Then I tried digging myself.

"I guess this is sort of fun, Grandpa," I told him.

"Sure it is," he said. "I knew you'd like it! And you're pretty good at it, too."

.. I couldn't stop my lips from curling up into a smile

tubular

13

Inference

What can you
infer from ...

I wandered far along the beach,
stopping now and then to shout
hello and wave at Grandpa ?

While I dug, Grandpa stood on the
beach and watched the sea. When
my bucket was nearly full, he rinsed
the clams in sea water. Then he
began digging for more clams to
fill up his own bucket.

After a while, I took off my sneakers
and walked along the shore, letting
the cool, wet sand ooze up between
my toes. I watched as the sea
water seeped into my footprints
and slowly turned them into small
pools. I wandered far along the
beach, stopping now and then to
shout hello and wave at Grandpa.
He waved back every time. Far
along the beach, I discovered all
sorts of ocean treasures.

. . . I wasn't so

I tucked a round, flat sand dollar into my pocket. I found a sea snail almost the size of my fist and tossed it into the rippling waves. I poked a stick at a dead jellyfish that looked like a broken balloon. I watched a crab scuttle sideways in the sand like a wind-up toy.

Then I sat down and started to build a castle in the damp sand.

Maybe the seashore isn't so bad after all, I thought.

But a while later, when I looked out across the sea, I wasn't so sure any more.

Setting Prediction

What do you think is going to happen to the setting? How might it affect Sophie?

sure any more

I poked a stick at a dead jellyfish that looked like a broken balloon.

What picture do you see in your mind?

Imagery

15

The Fog

PREDICT: What do you think will happen in this chapter?

Something strange was rolling towards me. Something billowy and white was gliding quickly across the surface of the sea, sailing towards me like a ghostly schooner.

"Sophie," Grandpa called. "Run back to me. Right now. The fog is rolling in!

"Run as fast as you can."

I started to run towards Grandpa in the distance, but the fog was too fast. It wrapped around me like a cold, wet sheet. Its clammy hands pressed against my face. The sun disappeared, and the beach became a cloud of swirling white. In a moment, Grandpa had vanished into the fog. I blinked fast so that I wouldn't cry.

"Grandpa," I yelled. "What should I do?"

"Stay where you are," he shouted back at me. "Don't wander off. Sit down on the sand and just stay put so I'll be able to find you."

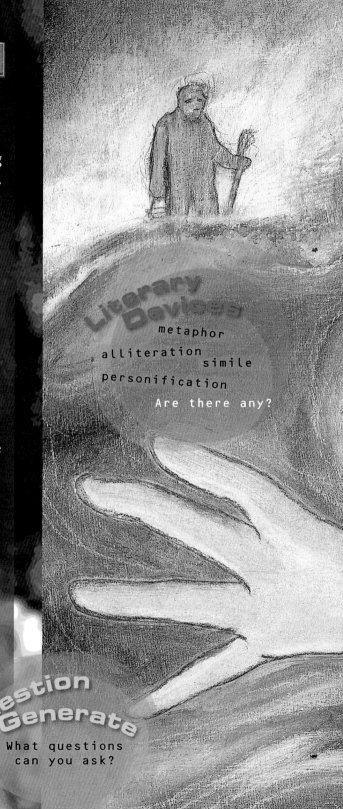

Literary Devices

metaphor
alliteration   simile
personification

Are there any?

Question Generate

What questions can you ask?

...a cloud of swirling white

Setting Analysis

How is the mood of the setting influencing the way Sophie is feeling now?

Grandpa...

Grandpa...

Inference

W h a t   c a n   y o u
i n f e r   f r o m . . .

I sat down hard in the
damp sand and waited **?**

18

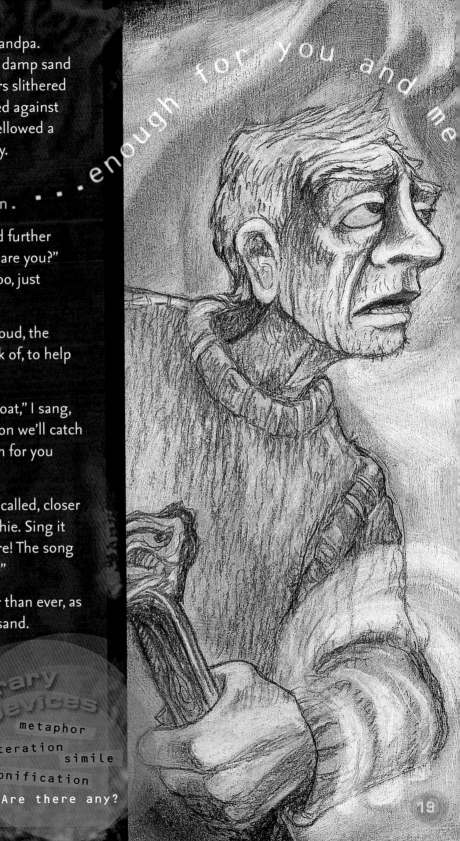

could hardly hear Grandpa.
sat down hard in the damp sand
nd waited. Fog fingers slithered
round me and pressed against
my skin. A fog horn bellowed a
warning across the bay.

'Grandpa!"
called again.

"Sophie?" He sounded further
away. "Sophie! Where are you?"
He sounded scared, too, just
ike me.

started singing out loud, the
first song I could think of, to help
Grandpa find me.

"Row, row, row your boat," I sang,
'swiftly out to sea. Soon we'll catch
a mess of fish, enough for you
and me!"

"Good girl," Grandpa called, closer
now. "Good idea, Sophie. Sing it
again. I'm almost there! The song
will help me find you!"

I sang it again, louder than ever, as
I sat shivering in the sand.

Literary Devices

metaphor

alliteration

simile

personification

Are there any?

...I thought you'd never find me

Suddenly, Grandpa appeared like a friendly phantom, stepping up to me out of the curling fog. I hugged him tightly. His scratchy whiskers felt familiar and good. He was shaking just like I was, so I hugged him harder.

"I was scared," I told him. "I . . . I thought you'd never find me."

I felt as if I was being swallowed up by that cold, wet fog.

"I was scared, too," said Grandpa. "Sometimes the sea can play tricks on you when you don't expect it. As I told you before, the sea can be a friend and an enemy. I've got our clams and your sneakers, Sophie. Put them on and we'll go home. I know the way."

Then Grandpa took my hand and led me home through the pillows of fog. The mumbling house was a welcome sight – so much safer than the smothering fog. It even seemed to be smiling at me with its sagging porch mouth. I smiled back.

"Soon the fog will roll back out," said Grandpa as we walked up the crooked steps. "Then the sea will be our friend again. But for now let's go inside, and I'll show you how to make clam chowder."

Question

How has the author shown a change in the relationship between Sophie and her grandfather?

...it even seemed to be smiling at me

Setting Analysis

How has the author shown that Sophie's attitude to the setting has changed from the beginning of the story?

The phone was ringing when we stepped inside. It was Mum. She asked how Grandpa and I were, and I told her about clam digging and how I got lost in the fog. Then Mum told me I was going to love the new house and my new bedroom. She said I could paint it any colour I wanted.

I was smiling when I hung up.

Inference

What inferences can you make about the character of Sophie's mum?

Hi, Mum.

Question

How has Sophie's attitude changed from the beginning of the story?

est soup ever tasted

I helped Grandpa rinse the sand out of the clams in the sink then put them in the big pot. Then he added water and put the clams on the stove to steam open. While they heated, we chopped the onions and diced potatoes. After the clams cooled off, I helped Grandpa pluck them out of their shells. Then he started to make clam chowder.

"You don't add the clams until the end, Sophie," Grandpa told me. He let me stir the bubbling chowder on the stove. It smelled really good.

Soon it was time for Grandpa to pour in hot milk and cream, and then I added the clams.

"Time to eat," said Grandpa.

It was the best soup I ever tasted. I ate three bowls.

Inference

What can you infer about the way Sophie is feeling from . . .

It was the best soup I ever tasted?

That night at bedtime, Grandpa sat in the rocker again and we sang the song together.

"Row, row, row your boat, swiftly out to sea. Soon we'll catch a mess of fish, enough for you and me."

And I was almost certain that I could hear Grandpa's old house mumbling right along with us as we sang.

ROW

Setting Comparison Chart

Compare the settings in Grandpa's Mumbling House.

Sophie's old house		?
The airport		?
Grandpa's house	Introduction of the story	?
	Middle of the story	?
	Conclusion of the story	?
The beach	Introduction of the story	?
	Middle of the story	?
	Conclusion of the story	?

Think about the Text:

Making connections

What connections can you make to the
emotions, settings, situations or characters of
Grandpa's Mumbling House?

feeling sad
and lonely

experiencing
family issues

being
judgemental

Text
to
Self

feeling
abandoned

experiencing
fear

feeling
insecure

feeling
secure

feeling
loved

Text to Text

Talk about other stories you have read that have similar features. Compare the stories.

Text to World

Talk about situations in the world that might connect to elements in the story.

Planning a Personal Recount

Planning

1 Think about an introduction.

WHO	Mum, Grandpa and me...
WHEN	One day...
WHERE	old house by the sea...
WHAT	I didn't want to go to Grandpa's house...

2 Think about events in order of time.

3 Think about . . .

including personal comments,

I wasn't so sure I liked the seashore.
I didn't want to go.

I missed my mum and dad.

I felt as if I was being swallowed up
by that cold, wet fog.

using the first person,

my   I   me   our   we

using the past tense.

When I arrived   I missed home

While I dug

4 Think about the conclusion.

Writing a Personal Recount

Have you . . .

- included your own responses and reactions?

- recorded the events in a sequence and made links to time?

- included events that all relate to one particular occasion, happening or idea?

- written a conclusion at the end that may have an interpretation of events or a personal comment?

- written your recount in the past tense?

- used the first person?

- personally involved yourself in the event?

Don't forget to revisit your writing.

Do you need to change, add or delete anything to improve your story?